New Beginnings

CELEBRATING BIRTH

ANITA GANERI

PETER BEDRICK BOOKS

NEW YORK

INTRODUCTION

In each of the world's six major religions, the most important times in a person's life are marked by special ceremonies. These are a bit like signposts on the journey through life, guiding a person from one stage of their life to the next. They also give people the chance to share their beliefs and their joys or sorrows, whether in celebrating a baby's birth, the change from child to adult, a wedding, or marking and remembering a person's death. For each occasion, there are prayers to be said, presents to give and receive, festive food to eat and stories to tell. Customs and ceremonies vary in different parts of the world. This book looks at just some of them.

CELEBRATING BIRTH

This book examines how people from the Hindu, Buddhist, Sikh, Jewish, Christian and Muslim faiths welcome a new-born baby into the world. You can find out how a baby's name is chosen and the meanings of popular names. You can also read about some very special birthdays.

In this book dates are written with BCE and CE, instead of BC and AD which are based on the Christian calendar. BCE means 'Before the Common Era' and it replaces BC (Before Christ). CE means 'in the Common Era' and it replaces AD (Anno Domini 'in the year of our Lord').

This is the Hindu sacred symbol 'Om'. It expresses all the secrets of the universe.

This wheel is a Buddhist symbol. Its eight spokes stand for eight points of the Buddha's teaching.

This Sikh symbol is called the 'Ik onkar'. It means 'There is only one God'.

The Star of David is a Jewish symbol. It appears on the flag of Israel.

The cross is a Christian symbol. It reminds Christians of how Jesus died on a cross.

The star and crescent moon are symbols of Islam.

CONTENTS

HONEY AND HOROSCOPES

In the Hindu religion, important times in a person's life are marked by 16 special ceremonies, called samskaras. These are performed in front of a sacred fire, while priests say prayers and read from the holy books. The first samskaras happen even before a baby is born, to give it the best possible start in life.

The baby is born

The birth of a baby is a happy time in a Hindu household. Soon after the baby is born, it is bathed and the sacred word, 'Om', is written in honey on its tongue, using a golden pen. 'Om' is a very holy word, recited at the beginning of prayers, blessings and meditation. It is believed to hold all the secrets of the universe.

At a Hindu naming ceremony, the father tells the priest the baby's name. The priest is wearing saffron robes, the holy colour of Hinduism.

Choosing a name

Twelve days after the baby's birth, the priest visits the family to bless and name the baby. The baby lies in its mother's lap, with its father to one side. In front of them is a metal plate spread with grains of rice. Using a piece of gold wire, the father writes the name of the family god and the baby's name and date of birth on the rice grains.

Then he whispers the baby's name into its right ear. The priest blesses the baby and shares out sweets and other offerings of food that he has blessed.

Casting a horoscope

Before the naming ceremony, the priest works out a horoscope for the baby, based on the position of the stars and planets at the time of its birth. From this, he reads the baby's future and suggests a suitable name.

This is the horoscope of a baby boy, written in Sanskrit, the ancient language of India.

A priest draws up a horoscope.

Some Hindu names

Many children are named after Hindu gods and goddesses, or have names with other religious meanings.

Boys' names
Suresh - another name for the great god, Shiva
Rabindra - son of Indra, the Lord of Heaven
Ram Kumar - son of the god, Rama
Sudarshan - another name for the blue god, Krishna

Girls' names
Vandana - prayer or homage
Radha - the name of Krishna's wife
Sita - the wife of Lord Rama
Lakshmi - the goddess of wealth and good fortune

The cycle of life

Hindus believe that when you die, your soul is reborn in another body, human or animal. You can be reborn many times, unless you break free from the cycle and reach moksha, or salvation. This is when your soul joins with the great soul, Brahman (God). It depends on your actions, and the results of your actions, in your present life. If you act well, you will be reborn in a higher form, closer to moksha. If you act badly, you will move further away. This process is called karma. This is the belief that all actions have their effects, good or bad.

This baby is having its first haircut. This is done to remove any bad karma. A prayer is said to wish the baby a long, happy and healthy life.

Showing the Sun

A few months after the naming ceremony, another samskara takes place, early in the morning. After praying to the family gods, the father takes his baby outside to see the rays of the rising Sun. The Sun is all-important, as the giver of life itself.

First haircut

Before the baby boy is a year old, the family gathers for another special event. First the priests perform a puja, or prayer ceremony. They sit in front of the sacred fire, reciting passages from the holy books. Then they draw a pattern in red dye showing the planets and the gods. The baby's parents make an offering – of water, flowers and incense – to each of these gods. Then the priests pour ghee (butter) on to the fire to make it blaze brightly. The puja ends with a joyful bhajan, or hymn. Everyone joins in.

After this the baby's hair is shaved off and collected for burning. This is believed to remove any bad karma from the baby's past lives (see box). The fire carries the offering of the hair up to the gods and wipes away evil.

The birth of the blue god

The blue god, Krishna, is one of the best-loved Hindu gods. His birthday is at midnight on the night of the full Moon in August. It is celebrated all over India with a festival called Janmashtami. This is the story of Krishna's birth.

Krishna's mother was a royal princess but the blue god did not grow up as a prince. His wicked uncle, the king, hated the child and vowed to kill him. Just in time, the gods warned Krishna's mother:

"Send your son across the river to live with Nanda, the cowherd."

So Vasudeva, Krishna's father, took his son to the banks of the Yamuna River. But the river was a raging torrent. How could they get across? Vasudeva put Krishna's basket down as he thought what to do.

Then Krishna, the blue god, poked a tiny foot out of his basket and dangled it into the water. At once the mighty river grew calm and parted, making a path for them to cross. For Krishna was no ordinary child.

THE BIRTH OF THE BUDDHA

Buddhists do not have set ceremonies to mark a baby's birth. Parents may take their babies to a temple to be blessed by the monks. For Buddhists, the happiest birthday of all is that of Prince Siddhartha Gautama. He went on to become the Buddha, whose teachings all Buddhists follow.

Greeted by the gods

In Nepal, about 2500 years ago, a baby was born in a grove of trees. A bright, full Moon shone in the sky. The gods showered the baby with sweet-smelling petals and poured scented water from heaven to bathe him. Then, as an earthquake shook the ground, the baby took seven steps forwards. The trees in the grove burst into flower. Blind people could see and lame people could walk again. Siddhartha Gautama, the Buddha-to-be, was born.

Soon afterwards Siddhartha's mother, Queen Maya, died. Siddhartha grew up in his father's, luxurious palace. A wise man gave his father a warning.

"Your son will become a great ruler or a great holy man," he said, "depending on how much suffering he sees in the world."

The king was determined that his son should rule after him. So he kept him safe inside the palace, surrounded by beautiful things.

One day, Siddhartha sneaked out of the palace, against his father's wishes. He saw three terrible sights – an old man, a sick man and a dead man. How badly they had suffered! Then he saw a monk, happy with his simple life. Siddhartha knew what to do. That night he left the palace for good, put on monk's robes and set off to follow this way of life.

Six years later, as he sat meditating under a tree, Siddhartha felt he understood the truth about suffering. He became the Buddha, a name which means 'awake' or 'enlightened', one of the greatest holy people of all. He spent the rest of his life travelling around India, teaching people a better, wiser way to live.

Buddhist monks meditate, just as the Buddha did.

Birthday bathday

In Japan, the Buddha's birthday is celebrated on 8 April with a festival called Hana Matsuri. Japanese people visit the temple to pour bowls of sweet tea over a statue of the Buddha. This reminds them of the Buddha's first bath (see page 10).

People pour sweet tea over a statue of the Buddha.

A WELCOME IN THE GURDWARA

For Sikhs, family life is very important. A baby is seen as a precious gift from God. To celebrate a baby's birth, the parents give boxes of sweets as presents to their friends and relations. In return, they receive gifts of money, new clothes and lengths of cloth for winding into turbans.

Words of prayer

Soon after the baby is born, the words of the Mool Mantar prayer (see box) are whispered in its ear. This is an important prayer. It sums up what the Sikhs believe about God.

The Mool Mantar

This prayer was composed by Guru Nanak, the founder of the Sikh religion.
'There is only one God
 Whose name is Truth
 God the creator
 is without fear
 is without hate
 is timeless and without shape
 is beyond death, the
   enlightened one
 and is understood through God's
   grace.'

A visit to the gurdwara

A few weeks after birth, parents take the baby to the gurdwara, the temple where Sikhs meet to worship. They want to thank God for the baby and to choose its name. They take with them a beautiful, embroidered silk cloth, called a romalla. It will be placed over the *Guru Granth Sahib*, the holy book of the Sikhs, to cover it when it is not being used. (You can read more about this book on page 14.) The baby's naming ceremony usually takes place at the end of a normal service in the gurdwara.

A close-up of a romalla, beautifully embroidered with red and gold thread

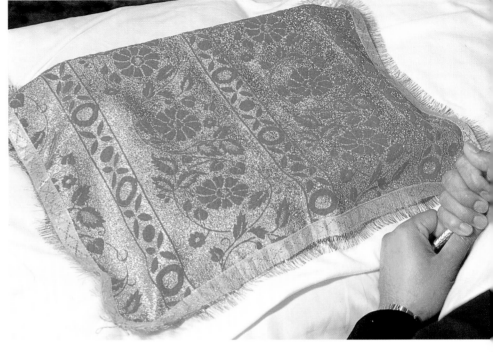

When it is not being read, the Guru Granth Sahib *is covered by a romalla of silk or velvet.*

The Sikh symbol

This Sikh symbol is called the 'Ik onkar' which means 'There is only one God', the first words of the Mool Mantar prayer. It is sometimes embroidered on romalla cloths.

The Guru Granth Sahib

The Sikhs' holy book is called the *Guru Granth Sahib*. It is a collection of hymns and prayers, written hundreds of years ago by the Sikh gurus, or teachers, and other holy people. In the gurdwara, the *Guru Granth Sahib* is treated with great respect. An appointed reader, called a granthi, looks after it and reads from it during services. It is placed on a raised throne under a canopy. When not in use, it is wrapped up in a romalla cloth.

Reading the Guru Granth Sahib

The Guru Granth Sahib *is written in Gurmukhi. This is the script used to write Punjabi, the Sikh language.*

Choosing a name

In the gurdwara, the parents and baby stand before the sacred book. An Ardas, a prayer, is said. Then the granthi opens the *Guru Granth Sahib* at random and reads the first word on the left-hand page. The parents choose a name for their baby which begins with the same letter as that word. They tell the granthi who announces the name to the congregation. In reply, and to show that they all agree, everyone shouts "Sat sri akal" which means "God is truth".

Joining in

At the end of the ceremony, everyone receives a portion of karah parshad, a sweet made from flour, sugar and butter. Sharing the food shows that everyone is equal in God's eyes. Sometimes a sweet, sugary mixture, called amrit, is dripped on to the baby's tongue, to give the baby a welcome into the Sikh community.

There is great celebration if a baby is born at the time of the Sikh winter festival of Lohri. The baby is bounced in a pile of sweets or popcorn, and sweets are given to friends and relatives.

Guru Nanak's birthday

Every year, in November, Sikhs all over the world celebrate the birthday of Guru Nanak, the founder of the Sikh religion. He was born in a small village in India in 1469. A special festival, called a gurpurb, is held in his honour. The most important part of the festival is the reading of the *Guru Granth Sahib*, non-stop from beginning to end. There is also a colourful procession through the streets, carrying a copy of the *Guru Granth Sahib* on a decorated platform called a palki.

Guru Nanak, the founder of the Sikh religion. When he was about 30 years old, God told him to go out and teach people the right way to live. He spent the rest of his life preaching and teaching.

A COVENANT WITH GOD

Jews do not believe in rebirth, as Hindus and Buddhists do. They believe that each life is a gift from God, to be lived according to God's commandments. According to Jewish law, anyone with a Jewish mother is a Jew, whether they follow the customs and practices of Jewish religion or not.

Brit Milah

Eight days after a baby boy is born a ceremony is held, called the Brit Milah. This can take place at home or in the hospital where the baby was born. Sometimes only men and boys are present. Sometimes the baby's mother watches too.

First, the baby is placed on a chair, known as Elijah's chair. Elijah was a Jewish prophet and a protector of children.

The father carries the baby on a cushion, ready for the Brit Milah ceremony. He says that he is presenting his son for circumcision, in keeping with God's wishes.

This seat is called Elijah's chair. The words on it mean welcome. The baby is placed here to gain Elijah's protection.

Then the baby is placed on his godfather's knee while a simple operation is carried out to cut a small piece of skin from his penis. This is called circumcision. It is performed by a specially trained Jew, called a mohel. It is quickly over.

A prayer

During the circumcision, the baby's father says a prayer:

"Blessed are you, Lord our God, King of the Universe, Who has blessed us with his commandments, and ordered us to enter my son into the promise made by Abraham."

Then the baby is given his name and more prayers are said to bless the child. Everyone drinks some wine – even the baby is given a drop – and a party is held to celebrate.

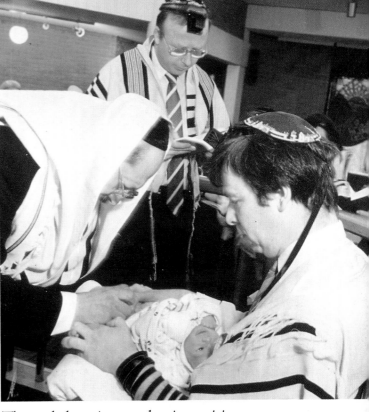

The mohel carries out the circumcision.

Jewish names

As well as their ordinary names, Jewish children are also given Jewish names, often of important Jews from history.

Boys' names
David - King of Israel in the 10th century BCE
Samuel - David's son
Jacob - the son of Abraham's son, Isaac
Aaron - brother of Moses. Jews believe that Moses was given the *Torah* by God.

Girls' names
Ruth - King David's great grandmother
Miriam - sister of Aaron
Sarah - Abraham's wife
Rebecca - Isaac's wife
Esther - a Persian queen who lived more than 2300 years ago. She saved the Jews living in Persia from death.

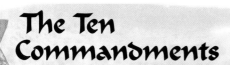

The Ten Commandments

The most important rules for Jews to follow are called the Ten Commandments. They believe that these were given by God to Moses.

1. I am the Lord your God.
2. You must have no other gods.
3. You must not misuse my name.
4. Keep the Shabbat day holy.
5. Respect your father and mother.
6. Do not kill.
7. Do not commit adultery.
8. Do not tell steal.
9. Do not tell lies
10. Do not be jealous of other people.

Copies of the Torah are handwritten in Hebrew on special scrolls. Writing out a Torah takes about a year. Hebrew is the sacred language of the Jews.

The Covenant

The Brit Milah ceremony is very ancient, originating more than 3000 years ago in the time of Abraham, the first Patriarch of the Jewish people. The Brit Milah initiates every Jewish male child into the covenant made between God and Abraham whereby God promises to make Abraham's descendants a great nation in a land given to them by God.

The birth of a daughter

There is no Brit Milah when a baby girl is born. Instead, she is taken to the synagogue on the first Shabbat (Saturday) after her birth. Her father is called up to the bimah, the raised platform at the front of synagogue. This is where the *Torah*, the Jewish scriptures, are placed to be read. Being called up is a great honour. While the father stands at the bimah, his daughter's name is announced to the congregation.

In the synagogue, the sacred Torah scrolls are kept in a special cupboard, called the Ark. This is the holiest part of the synagogue.

Five silver shekels

Another ceremony may be held when a first-born baby boy is about a month old. His father pays five shekels (silver coins) to the synagogue. This dates back to a time long ago in Israel. All first-born boys were given to God in thanks. They were sent to the Temple in Jerusalem to serve as priests or helpers. Later, it became the custom for parents to pay a sum of money in place of their son. Today, the money is usually donated to charity.

Shekels are still used in Israel.

BEING BAPTISED

When a Christian baby is born, its parents take it to church to be baptised. A service is held at which the baby is accepted into the Christian faith and given a name. Some close friends or relations are chosen to be the baby's godparents. They promise to help support and look after the child as it grows up in the Christian faith.

A baby is baptised at the font.

A shell is sometimes used to scoop water over the baby's head. This is a reminder that the first Christians were baptised by the river or the seashore.

Washing away sins

For the baptism, the parents and godparents stand near the font, a special container which holds holy water. In old churches, the font is often at the back of the church. It reminds worshippers entering the church that baptism is the first step on their journey through life. The priest, or minister, asks the parents and godparents to promise to look after the baby and to help them follow the teachings of Jesus Christ. Then he or she

pours some holy water over the baby's head and makes the sign of the cross on its forehead. The water is meant to wash away the baby's sin. The cross is the symbol of the Christian faith.

Baptising the baby

As the priest pours the water and makes the sign of the cross, he says the baby's name, together with the following words:

"I baptise you in the name of the Father, and of the Son, and of the Holy Spirit. I sign you with the Cross, the sign of Christ."

Baptism is sometimes called Christening when a person becomes a member of the Christian family. The baby's first name is also known as its Christian name.

The light of the world

In some churches, during the baptism, the priest hands a candle to the baby's parents. This is lit from the Paschal, or Easter, candle, near the altar. It is a symbol of Jesus as the light that will help to guide the baby through life. The priest gives the candle to a parent or godparent saying, "Receive this light. This is to show that you have passed from darkness to light." Everyone replies "Shine like a light in the world, to the glory of God the Father."

After the service, there is a party for friends and family. Some people save the top layer of their wedding cake to use at the party.

A Paschal candle. It is decorated with a cross and two letters which stand for Jesus Christ.

The priest lights the candles used at the baptism from the Paschal candle.

Chrismation

Orthodox Christians have an extra ceremony at the baptism. This is called Chrismation. The priest draws a cross in holy oil, or chrism, on the baby's head and chest. This is believed to protect the baby and give it strength. The oil is a symbol of the Holy Spirit, the invisible part of God which is believed to be present in everything.

This is a baptism in an Orthodox Church in Moscow. The small chest next to the font holds the bottles of holy oil, or chrism.

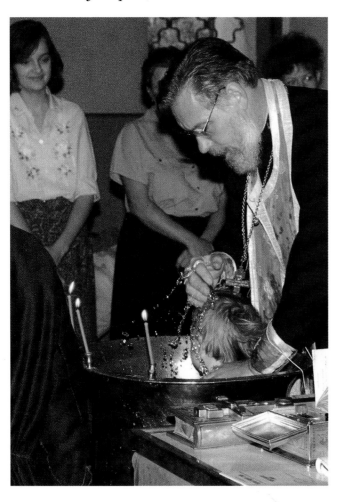

Saints' names

Many Christian children are named after saints. For example:

Boys' names
Christopher - patron saint of travellers
Antony - patron saint of lost objects
Dominic - patron saint of astronomers
Joseph - patron saint of carpenters

Girls' names
Teresa - patron saint of lacemakers
Anne - patron saint of grandmothers
Barbara - patron saint of architects
Catherine - patron saint of students

St Christopher

The birth of Christ

At Christmas, Christians all over the world celebrate the birth of Jesus Christ almost 2000 years ago. Christians believe Jesus is the Son of God, and follow his teachings and example.

Jesus's mother, Mary, and her husband, Joseph, had travelled to the small town of Bethlehem to pay their taxes. When they arrived, the town was crowded and they had to sleep in a stable. It was here that Jesus was born. News of Jesus's birth spread quickly, for the scriptures had told of a baby who would become the saviour of the world. The first visitors were shepherds who had been tending their flocks in the fields nearby. Angels told them about the baby and they wanted to see him for themselves. Next came the three wise men, bringing gifts of gold, frankincense and myrrh. They had followed a star to the stable.

Jesus's birthday is traditionally celebrated on 25 December, though no one knows exactly when he was born. Orthodox Christians celebrate Christmas on 6 January, the day on which the three wise men are said to have visited the stable.

THE CALL TO PRAYER

For Muslim parents, children are a gift from Allah (God), and looking after a baby is a special responsibility. From an early age, children are taught to be good Muslims, learning about their faith, working hard and caring for others.

First words

The first words that a Muslim baby hears are those of the Adhan, or call to prayer, whispered in its right ear. These are the words that sound out everyday from the mosque, calling Muslims to prayer:

"Allah is the greatest.
I bear witness that there is no God but Allah
I bear witness that Muhammad is the messenger of Allah.
Come to prayer
Come to safety
Allah is the greatest."

After this another prayer called the iqamah is whispered in the baby's left ear. This is usually done by the baby's father, or by the imam – the person who leads the prayers in the mosque.

This father is whispering the words of the Adhan into his new-born baby's ear.

A sweet start

Sometimes a tiny amount of sugar or honey is placed on the baby's tongue, and a prayer is said giving thanks to Allah. No one knows exactly why this is done. Some people say it links the sweet words with a sweet taste.

Names and gifts

When the baby is seven days old, the aqiqah ceremony is held. First the baby's hair is shaved off. Then the hair is weighed and the weight of the hair is given in silver to the poor. Often, money is given instead. Giving to the poor is one of the main beliefs of Islam (see page 27). At this ceremony, the baby is also given its name (see box below). All Muslim names have a meaning. Choosing a good name is very important!

Muslims praying in a mosque. Muslims must pray five times a day. This is one of the Five Pillars of Islam (see page 27).

Choosing a name

Muhammad was the prophet, or messenger, of Allah who first taught the religion of Islam in the 7th century CE (see page 27). Many Muslim children are named after him or after someone in his family, for example Amina, his mother, or Ibrahim, his son. Others are given one of the 99 names that Muslims use for Allah, for example Rashid, which means 'guide'.

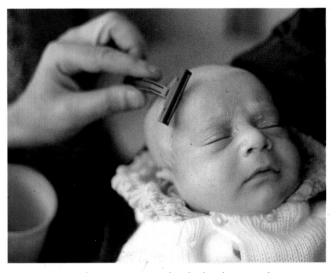

At its aqiqah ceremony, the baby has its hair shaved off.

Reading and studying the Qur'an *is very important for Muslim boys and girls.*

Time for a feast

After the aqiqah ceremony, the family hold a feast for their friends and neighbours. Traditionally, in Muslim countries two sheep or goats were killed for the feast if the baby was a boy; one if a girl was born. One-third of the meat was given to the poor. Today, though, it is often easier for people to give money instead.

The Bismillah

In some Muslim countries a ceremony, called the Bismillah, is held when a child is four or five years old. The child recites the first few verses of the *Qur'an*, the Muslim holy book, which have been learned by heart. The *Qur'an* is written in Arabic, the language spoken by Muhammad. The 'Bismillah' is said at the beginning of a task or a meal to ask for Allah's blessing. It means 'In the name of Allah, the merciful'.

The Bismillah, written in Arabic

The Qur'an *is written in Arabic the language spoken by Muhammad.*

The Five Pillars of Islam

The five main beliefs of Islam are called pillars because they help to 'support' Islam, just as real pillars support a building. They help Muslims to be aware of Allah in everything they do.

1. Shahadah, or the statement of faith. This says that: "There is no other God but Allah, and Muhammad is his prophet."
2. Salah, or prayer. Muslims must pray five times a day, at set times, facing the holy city of Mecca.
3. Zakah, or giving money to the poor. Muslims believe that this is their duty.
4. Sawm, or fasting. Muslims do not eat or drink from dawn until sunset during the Islamic month of Ramadan.
5. Hajj, or pilgrimage. Muslims try to make a pilgrimage to Mecca at least once in their lives.

Muhammad's early life

The prophet Muhammad was born in Mecca, Saudi Arabia, in 570 CE. His father, Abdullah, died before he was born. While Muhammad was still a baby his mother, Amina, sent him to be looked after by a foster-mother. That was the custom in those days. The woman who cared for Muhammad was called Halimah. She lived in a nearby village. She was very happy to take Muhammad home with her and loved him as her own son. Some years later, Muhammad went back to Mecca to live with his mother. But Amina died when he was just six years old. So Muhammad was brought up by his grandfather and, later, by his uncle. He learned to work hard and, when he grew up, he became a merchant like his uncle.

FACT FILES

 ## Hinduism

- **Numbers of Hindus:** *c.*732 million
- **Where began:** India (*c.* 2500 BCE)
- **Founder figure:** None
- **Major deities:** Thousands of gods and goddesses representing different aspects of Brahman, the great soul. The three most important gods are Brahma the creator, Vishnu the protector, and Shiva the destroyer.
- **Places of worship:** Mandirs (temples), shrines
- **Holy books:** *Vedas*, *Upanishads*, *Ramayana*, *Mahabharata*

Buddhism

- **Numbers of Buddhists:** *c.* 314 million
- **Where began:** Nepal/India (6th century BCE)
- **Founder figure:** Siddhartha Gautama, who became known as the Buddha
- **Major deities:** None, the Buddha did not want people to worship him as a god.
- **Places of worship:** Viharas (monasteries or temples), stupas (shrines)
- **Holy books:** *Tripitaka* (*Pali Canon*), *Diamond Sutra* and many others

Sikhism

- **Numbers of Sikhs:** *c.* 18 million
- **Where began:** India (15th century CE)
- **Founder figure:** Guru Nanak
- **Major deities:** One God whose word was brought to people by ten earthly gurus, or teachers.
- **Places of worship:** Gurdwaras (temples)
- **Holy book:** *Guru Granth Sahib*

 ## Judaism

- **Number of Jews:** *c.* 17 million
- **Where began:** Middle East (*c.* 2000 BCE)
- **Important figures:** Abraham, Moses, Isaac, Jacob
- **Major deities:** One God who created and rules over the world.
- **Places of worship:** Synagogues
- **Holy books:** *Tenakh* (Hebrew *Bible*), *Torah* (the first five books of the *Tenakh*), *Talmud*

Christianity

- **Numbers of Christians:** *c.* 2000 million
- **Where began:** Middle East (1st century CE)
- **Important figure:** Jesus Christ
- **Major deities:** One God, in three aspects – as the Father (creator of the world), as the Son (Jesus Christ), and as the Holy Spirit
- **Places of worship:** Churches, cathedrals, chapels
- **Holy books:** *Bible* (Old and New Testaments)

 ## Islam

- **Numbers of Muslims:** *c.* 1000 million
- **Where began:** Saudi Arabia (*c.* 610 CE)
- **Important figure:** The prophet, Muhammad
- **Major deities:** One God, Allah, who revealed his wishes to the prophet Muhammad.
- **Places of worship:** Mosques
- **Holy books:** The *Qur'an*

GLOSSARY

Adhan The words that call Muslims to prayer.

Allah The Arabic word for God.

amrit A special mixture of sugar and water used at Sikh ceremonies.

aqiqah A ceremony that takes places when a Muslim baby is about a week old. This is when the baby is given its name.

baptism A ceremony at which a person becomes a full member of the Christian Church. They are sprinkled or bathed in water as a sign that they are cleansed from sin.

bhajan A Hindu hymn or song of praise.

bimah A raised table or desk in the front of a synagogue. The *Torah* scrolls are placed on the bimah for reading.

Brit Milah The ceremony at which a Jewish baby boy is circumcised.

Chrismation Part of the baptism ceremony in an Orthodox church.

circumcision The cutting of a small piece of skin from a boy's penis. Jewish and Muslim boys are circumcised.

covenant A special agreement between God and the Jews.

font A container in a church which contains holy water for baptisms.

granthi A Sikh who is appointed to look after and read from the *Guru Granth Sahib*.

gurdwara A Sikh place of worship.

gurpurb A Sikh festival which celebrates the birth or death of a Sikh guru (teacher).

Guru Granth Sahib The holy book of the Sikhs.

horoscope A chart showing the position of the stars and planets at the time of a baby's birth.

Ik onkar A sacred Sikh symbol which means 'There is only one God'.

imam A Muslim person who leads the prayers in the mosque.

karah parshad A type of sweet food shared out at a Sikh ceremony.

karma Your actions and their results.

meditation Thinking deeply about something.

mohel A Jewish man trained to perform a circumcision.

moksha Freedom from being born over and over again.

Mool Mantar A very important Sikh prayer.

mosque A Muslim place of worship.

Om A sacred Hindu symbol and sound. It is thought to express all the secrets of the universe.

Paschal Another word for Easter.

puja A Hindu ceremony of worship.

Qur'an The holy book of the Muslims.

romalla An embroidered cloth which covers the *Guru Granth Sahib* when it is not being read.

samskara A ceremony which marks a special time in a Hindu's life. There are 16 samskaras in total.

Sanskrit An ancient Indian language. The Hindu sacred books are written in Sanskrit.

Shabbat The Jewish day of rest or worship. It lasts from sunset on Friday to sunset on Saturday.

shekel A Jewish silver coin.

Torah The Jewish holy book.

INDEX